Jumbo M

MW01045687

ABCs of Physics

An Introduction to the Language of Science

by A.C. Lemonwood

Jumbo Minds

Jumbo Minds, Inc., Rochester, NY

Published in the United States of America by Jumbo Minds, Inc. Rochester, NY USA

VISIT US AT JUMBOMINDS.COM

The publisher is not responsible for websites (or their content) that are not owned by the publisher.

Co-produced by **C. Knight**

Illustrations by **David Cowles**

Design by **Maria Friske**

Science Consultant **Paul Williams**

20 19 18 17 16 15   1 2 3 4 5

Proudly printed in the United States of America

SUMMARY: Introduces the English alphabet and the language and concepts of physics to young readers through short, precise definitions and colorful illustrations.

LCCN: 2015951179
ISBN: 978-1-944049-13-3 (PB)
LCC upon request   421′.1

The typeface used in the body of this book is OpenDyslexic 3, designed by Abelardo Gonzalez, 2012. This font has been used to increase readability.

This paper meets the requirements of ANSI/NISO z39.48-1992 (Permanence of Paper)

Books by Jumbo Minds, Inc.

Jumbo Minds' Science ABCs:
ABCs of Earth Science
ABCs of Chemistry
ABCs of Biology
ABCs of Physics

Preface

Welcome to Jumbo Minds' Science ABC books! To us, science is its own language. Studies show that the best time for children to learn additional languages is birth through age five. Exposure to a language during that time period of explosive brain growth leads to improved language fluency and understanding later in life.*

Our goal is to increase children's scientific literacy and share our love of science. To accomplish this, Jumbo Minds is introducing the language of science to growing minds. Turn these pages and make some brain connections! Enjoy exploring the world of science!

*Others agree:
"The National Science Teachers Association (NSTA) affirms that learning science and engineering practices in the early years can . . . lay the foundation for a progression of science learning in K–12 settings and throughout their entire lives."

Reprinted with permission from the NSTA position statement, Early Childhood Science Education

Physics is the study of how matter and energy relate to each other, such as motion, force, and light.

Acceleration

speeding up, slowing down, turning

In physics, the word acceleration means more than its common use in everyday life. Acceleration is when a moving object speeds up, slows down, or turns.

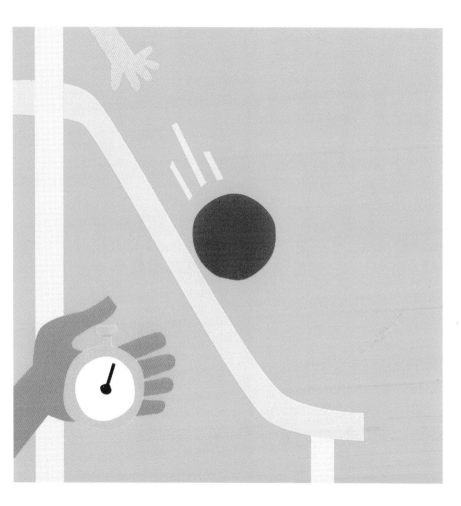

Bb

Buoyancy
floating force

A force is a push or pull on an object that can cause or prevent motion. Buoyancy is the force that pushes up to keep an object floating on liquid while the force of gravity is pulling down.

Cc

Centripetal Force
circular force

A force pulling a revolving object toward the center of a circle. Quickly swinging around a bucket full of water, without the water spilling, creates centripetal force. The centripetal force pulls the bucket toward the body; without that force, the bucket would move away in a straight line.

Decibel

sound measurement

A scale used to measure the intensity of sound waves. A low decibel (dB) reading shows a quiet sound, and a high decibel reading shows a loud sound. Whispering is about 30 dB, while shouting is around 85 dB.

Einstein
famous scientist

A famous German-American physicist. Albert Einstein is famous for many ideas, including the theory of relativity ($E = mc^2$). This theory explains how movement is relative to other objects using energy (E), mass (m), and the speed of light (c).

Ff

Friction

rubbing

A force between two surfaces that slows the movement of an object. Low friction surfaces allow an object to move easily. Because there is less friction on ice, pushing a large object on an icy lake is much easier than pushing it on a grassy surface.

Gg

Gravity

downward pull

A force that pulls everything toward the center of the earth (or toward the center of any large object in outer space). If we did not have gravity on earth we would float.

Hh

Horsepower
power measurement

Power is how quickly energy is used (how quickly work is done). Horsepower is used to measure the power of large machines, like truck and tractor engines. One horsepower (hp) is the power needed to raise 550 pounds (about the size of a male tiger) a distance of one foot in one second.

Inertia

resistance to change in motion

Inertia is when an object wants to stay in motion or stay at rest. A bicycle rider has inertia and will keep moving even if the bike stops.

Jj

Jet Propulsion

opposite push

A thrust (powerful push) in one direction caused by a blast of liquid or gas in the opposite direction. When the force created by a rocket engine pushes down, the rocket will move up. Jet propulsion is explained by Newton's 3rd Law (for every action there is an equal and opposite reaction).

Kinetic Energy

energy of motion

The energy an object has because it is moving. A playground swing in motion has kinetic energy.

Light
waves and particles of energy

A wave of energy that contains tiny particles called photons and travels in a straight line. Types of light include infrared, visible, and ultraviolet. Humans can only see visible light; white light from our sun actually contains all colors such as red, orange, yellow, green, blue, and violet.

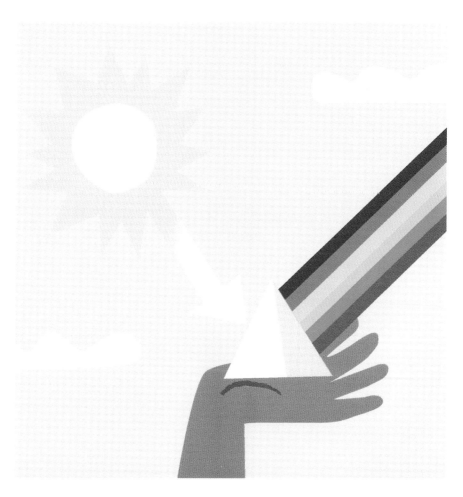

Mm

Magnet
magnetic field source

An object with an invisible zone, called a magnetic field. Magnets have poles (north and south) and attract magnetic materials such as iron nails. Many electronic devices and motors use magnets to work.

Newton's Laws of Motion
universal motion laws

<u>First Law</u> – An object at rest tends to stay at rest and an object in motion tends to stay in motion (with the same direction and speed) unless acted upon by a force.

<u>Second Law</u> – The more mass an object has, the more force is needed to accelerate it.

<u>Third Law</u> – For every action there is an equal and opposite reaction.

Oo

Optics
study of light

The study of the behavior of light (such as visible, infrared, and ultraviolet), and how light interacts with matter. Some optic scientists and engineers study lasers.

Pp

Potential Energy
stored energy

The energy an object at rest has because of its position. When a playground swing is pulled back, but is not yet in motion, it has potential energy. Once movement starts, the energy becomes kinetic energy.

Qq

Quasar

high-energy space region

An area in space that is powered by a black hole and emits large amounts of energy and light. Quasars are often created by colliding galaxies.

Reflection

bouncing light rays

The action when a light ray bounces off a surface. When light rays hit the surface of an object, some rays are absorbed and some are reflected. The colors that we see are the reflected light rays. The red apple absorbs all light rays except red, which is reflected.

Ss

Speed
how far, how fast

The distance an object travels in an amount of time. The speed of a marathon runner or an automobile can be measured in kilometers per hour (km/h) or miles per hour (mph).

Tt

Trough
wave bottom

The lowest point of a wave. The opposite of the trough is the crest (highest point of the wave). The trough is a part of waves we can see, like water waves, and also part of waves we cannot see, such as sound, x-rays, and light waves.

Uu

Universe
everything in space

All matter and space including dust, stars, planets, clouds, life, and galaxies; also known as the cosmos

Vibration
back and forth

Repeated back-and-forth motion. The movement of a plucked guitar string causes the air to vibrate, creating sound waves that can travel to our eardrums.

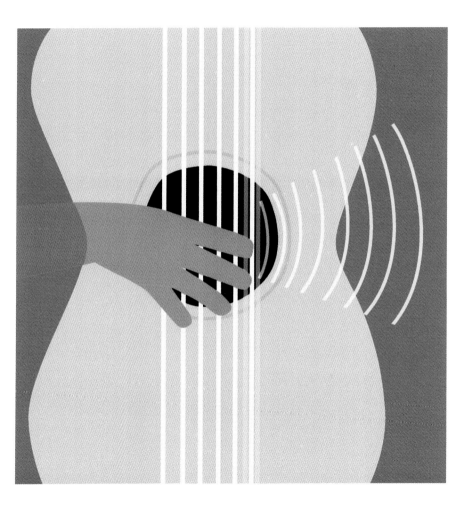

Watt
unit of power

Work done or energy used in a certain amount of
time. Watts are often used to measure the power
needed to push an electric current through a resisting
object (like a light bulb). Some light bulbs have a
measurement of 60 watts (W) or 100 W.

X-axis
horizontal graph line

Scientists use graphs to organize information and show patterns. The x-axis is the horizontal line on a graph, and is often used to show measurement or location.

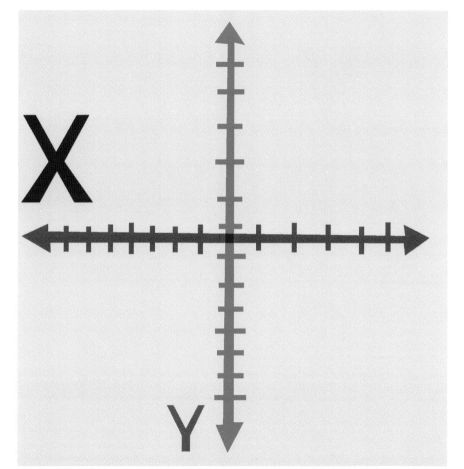

Yy

Light-Year

distance light travels in a year

A light-year measures distance, not time. Light travels 300,000 kilometers (186,000 miles) in one second! Astronomers have measured one light-year as about 9.5 trillion km (6 trillion miles). The closest star to our sun is a little more than 4 light-years away.

Zz

Absolute Zero
lowest temperature

Absolute zero is the lowest possible temperature. Scientists think atoms will not move at that temperature. Lord Kelvin developed the idea of absolute zero based on the Celsius (C) temperature scale. Absolute zero is equal to 0 K (Kelvin) and about − 273°C.